Epoch

poems by

Paul Fauteux

Finishing Line Press
Georgetown, Kentucky

Epoch

ACKNOWLEDGMENTS

Thanks to *After the Pause* for publishing "Quondam," "Mining,"
"Fireplace," and "Thirty."

Publisher: Leah Maines
Editor: Christen Kincaid
Cover Art: Brenna Killeen
Author Photo: Jessica Fauteux
Cover Design: Elizabeth Maines McCleavy

Printed in the USA on acid-free paper.
Order online: www.finishinglinepress.com
           also available on amazon.com

Author inquiries and mail orders:
Finishing Line Press
P. O. Box 1626
Georgetown, Kentucky 40324
U. S. A.

Table of Contents

Age

The terror of roiling age
is only that the lines
we left for redress
are long-dried, their paper
musty, and more kind eyes
bespeckle the blue-black
from which we've floated beacons:
little paper lamps
most beautiful
in an empty sky.

Subordinance

If no one comes to drink with me, the gravitons comprising
Pluto's plutoid orbital tendency (mass?) go undiscovered or ill-
understood, and available modes of thought cohesion falter also.
Breads, as we've come to know them, will de-yeast and come up
wonder-less in the face of diminished call for cordial revelry, of
which breads are part and parcel, too. The to-go menu batters
the imagination into dumb subordinance, hovering inches from
the red-brick wall in the dim iridescence of barroom's brittle
firmament.

Conflict

When there's a food truck,
buy from it. The pork
will be OK, and hot sauce
rescues anything. There isn't really
an elevator with two sides,
where one side is the "crime
elevator" which stops a shimmy-
climb away from an abandoned
children's playhouse suite,
and also stops at an otherwise
inaccessible train station servicing
off-grid big box stores or secret
executive pools, and you won't
show the blond from work
the children's rooms the day
your wife declined the invitation
to stay and work on contracts,
but that'd be pretty cool: feeling
conflicted.

Cut Loose

"To cut loose" means
"to come away empty handed,"
that you've come to think of it
differently, and that the peace
you wanted in the clearing
with walking paths and deer
bedding in the tall grass
was *anicca*, sinuating sands
in the desultory winds.

Hajj

If no one comes to drink with me, the Hajj just won't get started.
We'll exuberate in mundane things; I'll see the little dimple on
your leather handbag where the bronze loop is sewn into folds
of hide gather the space the handbag leaves behind. On May 29,
1453, the last Byzantine fell at the city walls, battling Mehmed.
He spit into his eye and offered commandaria in a cup, saying he
was "clay-brained guts" and a "knotty-pated fellow."

Patio

The same girl always
walks the wide sidewalk
past the little bushes
while the cool breeze
bungles through my button
shirt—loose khakis,
tossed black hair thrown
over-sized button-down
and opened top-two buttons,
opaque, black sunglasses on
sun-kissed skin, light impenetrable
as the deep black sea.

Representation

Say it, keep it.
Our laboratory
experiments maintain
our design is sound.

Stuff light hypotheses
down into your gut;
some kid will come around
with brand-new energy

so your schemes
stay private. Pens'
effete aspects row our feebler emblems
left to mindless right—

talk about ~~the way~~
things, go. The Dao
is one example; a second
ago, that was our best work.

Grass Spider

I, expecting father,
speak with cinders—

retreat into the forest enclave
abutting rushing cars:

lollybolly pine, cicadas and
easter cottonwood—

clear between the asphalt
footpath's rubbled end

and un-mown septic field.
I run a little deeper—

sink to shoelace-depth
in sopping mud.

You've seen the grass spider.
His web has no adhesion,

so he runs in nimble poise—
plunging fangs and paralytic toxin

to cut the cut-and-run.

Wreck

People don't know what they're fucking doing. I could use a pull-up bar, whenever I get really jazzed I could do like ten pull-ups, and get really built without all the shakes and gyms and personalities and impressing women and real-sun tans. Every time I wreck a car, the wind blows bitter and there is a single crow up on the transformer box in a pale grey sky.

Letter to my son

Hey. On August 13th,
seven months out, I drove
department store to department store
searching for natural wood charcoal.
I bought a gyro from a Greek
man whose wife bustled in
to the empty restaurant
to say something about the kids.
I bought some German pilsner
and made my way home, where I resolved
to place a beer-laden mini fridge
in every room with a good enough
chair, or desk, or sofa.

Quondam

Fukushima.

You—the rolling *than*
smooth peaks; little

grey buildings
in fine fog; fat children,

dithery indoors
for the irradiated soccer field.

You, and the grey-hard bank
of Abukuma River.

My wife bewails
our enervated town, the sandstone

creeks with skipping rocks
and bamboo thicket.

No, the thicket's gone.

I go to work in coat
and hat. My belly grows—

our cats heed not
the gentle lamp,

the warm orange table.

Letter to my daughter

Last night, your mother passed
a difficult test, whereupon
I fell into a deep blue depression
since I was so isolated and had failed
so very many times. I became
non-communicative, slept, and dreamed
I'd eaten soft, delicious magnets
belonging to Ringo Starr, for which
I made reparations in an old blue
music shop which sold such magnets
which were commonplace in Brit-pop
drumming.

Thirty

You know,
the bubbling up sensation—
being thirty and holding
a washcloth—

remembering that as a child,
the cloth must have been super-
cloth: a sub-maranian
towel with super

duck-like properties,
but you are in a body now
like a consignment dresser—
re-tightening drawer knobs

and wondering whether
to re-finish or paint over.
You'll pry the lid
off an old paint can,

and find, inside,
an apricot.

Letter to my son

Hey. You might not read this,
but whatever. I didn't read much
when I was in your state, either.
Everyone I know is out of shape,
now. It's not a thing, really,
and it doesn't make a stirring
image, but you should know
that if you're gonna do it,
really, breathe it through the whole
of you, draw it through your crown
and to your toes and fill
the space and flutter in the
grass, not green or yellow
here

Mining

Autumn's thinning (is)
deep winter's augur—

rude poems bleed neither
sight, greed, nor Dao— "we

paid for the high room,
declaimed our worry which crept

from our hands
And gave us manners, calm, our soul, and room.

The wind is like a star; it tumbles, ebbs,
and glances leaves across the coarse black stone.

We dwell apart; the lowliest of duties
are fine and fine and done. A fire burns,

but that is not the point. The winds are strong,
and rains disjoin unsullied Autumn's clime.

Letter to my daughter

I tried to kill your mother
and give you three heads.
I tried unconsciously—
our table's Polyurethane
wanted further coating.
A part of me, though,
wanted three heads for you—
like Hecate, mixing herbs
in marble arches, necromancing
where appropriate—cosmic
mother-angel watching
our little family, reaching
land and sea and air.

Birth

Female lions give birth
to dead lions, who remain
dead for three days
until their father comes
and breathes into their faces.

Formed lions are formless;
we lick them into shape.

Fireplace

I'll tell you how to be better
in the time that you have

left: arrange your sofas
so the fire burns well.

When we sit at table,
we'll find comfortable distance

from each other. We'll bug
a stained-glass window, pane it

with cherry wood, and depict
the nonsense bird with seven

little flames, a long flag
emerging from a small box.

There's nothing inspiring about this:
wringing hands and hoping

little shelves will bear the weight
of our assorted vases.

People talk about music.
They always say "it's like

a gallop through a forest,"
which only works if it's been burned

back annually and there is space
between surviving oaks

and the Powhatan sit on river rafts
to watch the foliage burn—

the dusk alight in orange glow.

Alignment

Remember, you want
to be an old man
with perfect posture. That's
what all of this is for—
your lint-free shirt
hanging from your shoulders
as a wool-twist tapestry
on a grey-stone wall.
My father's Carrera
his feet won't drive
has a beautiful engine—
red with rust
at up-curled paint.

Yes yes sir

Yes yes sir
stay active
you'll keep caterwauling

when other sounds drop out

You'll announce arrivals,
set clear terms, and

ring long vowels with violent thunder

I find myself playing snakes

and ladders   my daughter
inspires awe in those around
who are inspired to do—

to find the best way

Paul Fauteux lives in Northern Virginia with his wife and two-year-old daughter. He teaches English at George C. Marshall High School. He cut his teeth at poetry open mics at the now-defunct art space/coffee house The Soundry in Vienna, published his first chapbook with Plan B press, and received his MFA in Creative Writing from George Mason University (in more or less that order) before marrying Jesse, who taught him how to throw pottery. Now he spends his days grading papers, raising his daughter, and compiling the Blue Apron recipes his wife enjoys in a three-ring binder.

Here is a partial list of items in his basement: a tricycle, dusty books, a mini-fridge, a princess-castle playset, a wooden sword, an L-shaped sofa, a small bottle of linseed oil, an electric drill, and a wooden kung fu dummy. A more extensive list is available from his credit card company.